CHRISTIAN FAITH
AND
POLITICAL CHOICE

by

JOHN C. BENNETT

THE RYERSON PRESS - TORO

FOREWORD

Here is the thirteenth series of lectures given at Queen's University under the Trust established in the name of the late Honourable Charles A. Dunning, Chancellor of Queen's University from 1940 to 1958. The purpose of the Chancellor Dunning Trust, founded in 1948, is "to promote understanding and appreciation of the supreme importance of the dignity, freedom and responsibility of the individual person in human society." It is a condition of the Trust that the Trustees of the University shall every three years determine the means by which the purposes of the Trust shall be pursued. So far, the method selected has been an annual series of lectures given at the University during the academic session. Normally, three formal lectures, supplemented by a considerable number of informal talks and discussions with students and staff, make up the programme.

Early in 1963 Dr. John C. Bennett, Dean of Union Theological Seminary, New York, gave the most recent series of lectures: "Christian Ethics and Political Decisions," "The Conflict of Ideologies in the Cold War," and "Christian Ethics and the Nuclear Dilemma."

The subject is of the first importance: it is the nature of power in the modern world and how it should be used. We live in a world in which power, and especially the power of states, permeates everything, and threatens to make our planet an ash heap. The use to be made of this devastating power rests on political decisions, for which, in a democracy, all citizens must share responsibility. For Christians, affirming the sacredness of human life, whether of enemy or friend, decisions to use nuclear weapons present a moral dilemma of almost paralyzing difficulty. We in the western democracies, having taken up nuclear arms to deter aggression, know that deterrence depends on being clear— and making clear—that we are not running a bluff. We know too that to use these weapons in a general war would destroy everything the strategy of deterrence is designed to protect. This is the awesome dilemma to which Dr. Bennett addresses himself as he deals with the issues of power in these lectures.

For many years, Dr. Bennett has reflected with urgent Christian concern on social and political problems. His Kingston listeners were moved and instructed as he took them through the stark issues of the hour with unflinching candour. Queen's University is glad to share with others the studied thought of a generous mind.

J. A. CORRY,
Principal.

Queen's University at Kingston,
May 9, 1963

PREFACE

This book contains the 1963 series of Chancellor Dunning Trust Lectures at Queen's University as delivered except for minor additions and editorial changes. It deals with some of the questions often raised about the political responsibility of Christians and about the Christian ingredient in complex political decisions. The second and third chapters illustrate the process of thinking about political issues in Christian terms by discussing two of the most baffling and most fateful problems of our time.

I am most grateful to Queen's University for the invitation to give these lectures. The faculty and students of Queen's have a remarkable way of receiving a visitor into its many-sided life. I shall never forget their kindness and the stimulus of the more than thirty engagements which they arranged for me during my two-week visit. I want especially to thank Principal and Mrs. Corry, Professor and Mrs. Donald Mathers and Professor and Mrs. A. J. Coleman for many acts of hospitality. Professor Mathers representing the field of Theology and Mr. J. A. W. Gunn of the Department of Political Science took great care in planning my schedule and were my chief guides as I moved from group to group on the campus. It would overburden this preface to name the many others to whom I am indebted for kindness and hospitality.

The third lecture was based upon an address to the convention of the Religious Education Association in Chicago in 1963 which was printed in the March-April number of *Religious Education*. I am grateful to the Rev.

Preface

Herman E. Wornom, Executive Secretary of the Association, for permission to publish the material in this book.

It was a matter of interest to me to visit the city of Kingston in 1963 in a different role and on my own volition because it happened that I was born there in 1902 when my parents were summer residents.

JOHN C. BENNETT

Union Theological Seminary,
New York City,
April 25, 1963

CONTENTS

I

CHRISTIAN ETHICS
AND POLITICAL DECISIONS

I have chosen as the general subject of these lectures an area
of concern that has great importance for the interest of the
Chancellor Dunning Foundation in "the dignity, freedom
and responsibility of the individual person in human
society." Many of the most fateful problems that affect the
individual person are political problems. They have to do
with the way in which our organized communities decide
to use power. The very processes of decision are in large
measure political processes. Increasingly the decisions that
we make about the direction of economic development are
made in the arena of politics. In this lecture I shall speak
about some of the broader issues that arise when we ask how
the moral judgments which are inspired by Christian Faith
are related to contemporary political decisions, and here I
shall have in view the kind of situation which we have in
both your country and mine, a situation that has these two
characteristics: (1) both countries are profoundly influenced
by the Christian tradition, so that at least there is some
meaning in the reference to a Christian conscience among
the citizens; and (2) both countries have democratic institutions that give Christian citizens, as well as other citizens,
opportunities to influence national decisions. We may all
be highly critical of the way in which these democratic
institutions work, but we can be very thankful that they do
work reasonably well; they are not frustrated by mass
illiteracy, by pervasive corruption or by conflicts so deep
that they threaten civil war or absolute stalemate.

Why is there any problem about relating Christian morality to political decisions? Have not Christians been doing this since the fourth century? Are not most of the morally alert Canadians and citizens of the United States Christians of a sort? There is much talk of Christian morality in Washington and in Ottawa. In Washington, indeed, both President Roosevelt and President Eisenhower thought it appropriate to lead the nation in prayer over the radio— each on one occasion. President Truman said on several occasions that his policy was based upon the Sermon on the Mount—apparently he believed this to be the case when he decided to have the atomic bomb dropped on Japan! You may have heard what a great commotion there was south of the border when the United States elected a Roman Catholic for president. Most of our official religion is expressed in such a way as to obscure the problem that I raise.

I shall begin by mentioning five difficulties that are present whenever we seek to move directly from Christian morality to politics.

The first, and probably the one that creates the most permanent problems, is the fact that there is a very great distance between Christian love as understood in the New Testament and the world of political power. This is true of love that does not count the cost to self, love that is always willing to go the second mile, love that forgives seventy times seven. How is such love to be related to the responsibilities of the statesman who is a trustee for the national interest? Christian advice to such responsible politicians must on the face of it seem irrelevant. Christians who have been most possessed by Christian love have often withdrawn from the responsibilities of citizenship. At one time they went off into the desert to escape these and many other compromises with the world. Often they went into monasteries. Sometimes they formed detached communities which they tried to make self-sufficient, and then they found that they had to migrate from country to country to find places where they would be let alone. Still other Christians have remained in the world but have decided to separate themselves from the military activities of the state. Others have made a sharp distinction between their Christian life and the harsh realities of the public order. While they have tried to do the will of God in both, they have kept to a minimum any influence from distinctively Christian love on their public duties; they have allowed a double standard to harden as between church and nation and as between the Christian in his personal life and the Christian as citizen. The statement of this approach has been clearest on Lutheran soil; perhaps others have often been more hypocritical or confused. I have said enough to suggest that there is indeed a problem here. And I believe that it is a problem with which all Christians will have to live and for which there is no fully satisfying solution. I shall have something to say about this in all of my lectures, though perhaps the clearest statement of my response to it will come in my last lecture when I deal with the nuclear dilemma.

A second difficulty is the political indifference of the New Testament. This indifference can be explained in part by the historical situation. The first-century Christians had no political power or responsibility. Moreover, they expected an early end of human history, and this made it natural for them to concentrate on the redemptive events that had so recently changed the face of the world for them and on the Kingdom that was to come by act of God. There may have been something providential about the fact that the New Testament writers were not concerned about political programmes for Palestine or for some larger part of the Mediterranean world in the first or second centuries. If such programmes were a considerable part of the substance of the Christian scriptures, we might be bound to a political legalism that would be quite irrelevant to our changing world. Perhaps we should be handicapped on a wide range of issues by accidental first-century ideas about politics, just as the church is often handicapped even now by some of St. Paul's accidental injunctions about the place of women in the church.

The third difficulty is of an entirely different sort. I refer here to the way in which the very success of Christianity as a religious movement in the western world has obscured the radical nature of Christian morality. We are often reminded of the historical dynamism of biblical religion and of the Christian tradition in contrast to many other religious traditions. This dynamism has meant that Christianity had a very great part in the formation of communities, finally of national communities, and of civilization in Europe. And the effects of this civilization-creating power of Christianity have, of course, spread to other continents, including our own. This is obvious enough, but think of one consequence of it. Christians found themselves at the top of these communities and of this civilization. They became the men of power and wealth. In many cases they lost the capacity to see the world from the point of view of the poor and the oppressed. Those who were close to power and privilege wrote most of the books of theology and ethics. The result of this has been that the great churches and their thinkers have not been free to bring radical Christian criticism to bear upon the political institutions of the west, and they have been especially handicapped in dealing with the moral problems of modern industrial society. Within the past seventy-five years there has been a momentous change for the better with regard to these matters, but it came very late—almost too late.

The fourth difficulty is in emphasis quite modern. This is the fact that most of the political problems of our time involve, together with moral issues about which there should be some Christian guidance, technical issues for which there is no Christian guidance at all. Often the relation between the moral factors and the technical factors may itself be a matter of controversy. An obvious example of such a controversy is the debate over nuclear tests. Also, there are issues of another sort that have always been present. We might call them prudential issues or strategic issues. Technical experts may not be the best judges of these. They require the kind of practical wisdom that comes from experience and responsibility. The politician at his best is extremely important in relation to such judgments. Most judgments of foreign policy today involve a combination of some expert knowledge about the forces at work in other nations with the best prudential judgments available based to a considerable extent on guesses—we hope, informed guesses. There are forms of wisdom which come from Christian sources, and I shall speak of these later. But the important point is that Christian sources of wisdom are not self-sufficient in relation to any of our political decisions.

The fifth reason for our present difficulty in seeing how Christian morality is related to political decisions is also modern. It is the fact that our nations are religiously pluralistic. There is no Christian nation, and no Christian government responsible to a Christian nation. Christians must work with adherents of other religions, and even more, in your country and mine, with people who have rejected all traditional religious commitments. Christians must work with Jews, but this creates few problems in social ethics, for Jews and Christians share the social ethic of the Old Testament. The decisions of a community, of a political party or of a government, in so far as they are grounded in morality, must be based upon broad principles of justice, upon moral sensitivities that are found among citizens of varying ultimate commitments. It is difficult to measure the extent to which in such countries as Canada and the United States these common moral convictions and sensitivities are the effect of a diffusion of Christian influences in the culture. To a considerable extent they are. But we must also recognize that churches have often benefited from the pressure of critics from outside. The conventional morality of Christians can become very smug, especially when they have the psychology of the majority. Jews in the United States often have a greater concern for justice for all minorities because they are themselves a minority. Whatever may be the ultimate moral stimulus that the Gospel has brought into western culture, very often elements of Christian ethics that are combined with a spirit of rebellion against the church and against the dominant powers in society have forced Christians to face realities which they would have preferred to ignore. I am not troubled about the moral effects of our religious pluralism. It forces Christians out of pious ruts. I doubt if the churches left entirely to themselves would ever have come to see with full clarity that it is best for a society that people have freedom to be wrong even about religious truth. I doubt whether, without much prodding from secular movements of protest, the churches would have come to take seriously the claims of more equal justice in economic life.

Look back over these five difficulties in relating Christian morality to politics. The first—the remoteness of Christian love from the world of power—will always be with us. There is no over-all solution for the problem which it raises; we must live with it with faith and perplexity. The second— the political indifference of the New Testament—can be explained. To the extent to which our period provides opportunities for political action by Christians that were not present in the first century, we need not be inhibited by it. It may even help to sustain the church under totalitarian regimes. Of the third—the way in which the success of the church has obscured the radical implications of

Christian social ethics—we may say that the excuse for it has passed for reasons which I shall soon explain. The fourth and fifth difficulties—the complex nature of political judgments and the religious pluralism of our nations—are both very much with us. They describe the conditions under which we must do our thinking and deciding, but they do not cancel the responsibility of Christians to think and decide in the political sphere.

Now I shall speak of two circumstances that should govern our thinking about Christian political responsibility. The first is not new, but it makes many situations in Christian history, including our own, different from that of the first century. Christians today in many countries have political power. They cannot leave political decision to rulers who stand over against them. It was natural for Paul to stress a political ethic of obedience to rulers. This obedience could not be absolute as long as Christians realized that they were to obey God rather than men, but except in rare cases of conflict of conscience, as in the case of the book of *Revelation* in the New Testament, obedience was sufficient. The thirteenth chapter of *Romans*, which begins with the words, "Let every person be subject to the governing authorities," has provided the proof text for the ethic of political obedience for nearly twenty centuries. But it is not difficult to see that when the people become the source of political authority, when there are no governing authorities set over them without their consent, this ethic of obedience is no longer adequate. Instead there must be emphasis upon responsibility for and participation in government by Christians themselves, in co-operation with their fellow-citizens. It is true that there are times when an individual confronts a law which he would prefer to disregard; then, unless there is involved an unusual conflict of conscience, he ought to obey the law. But this law is not wholly alien to him if he gives his consent to the processes by which it is enacted and enforced. The political responsibility of the Christian citizen in many nations, including our two nations, grows out of his political opportunities, his sharing of political power, his chance to do something to influence public opinion and the policies of government. I have said that this is not new, for in varying degrees Christians have had political power in other periods. It is the second circumstance that is new.

I refer here to the fact of rapid social and cultural and political change and especially to one aspect of this change, the capacity of almost every human group in our time to gain a hearing, to call attention to the injustices and oppression and deprivation from which they suffer. This is true of the economically poor, of the coloured races, of the peoples that have been subject to colonial powers.

It is not for us to decide whether or not there is to be change. The only course open to us is to do something to guide the change that is taking place. We may find ourselves giving it a kind of negative guidance by our own default. This new circumstance makes impossible one of the most common Christian attitudes toward politics: a complacent and pious acceptance of the *status quo*. We can no longer say to ourselves what Christians have often said to themselves in the past: "Things could be better, but our society has been like this for a long time and it is not intolerable (especially for the class of people who can be articulate about it). Let us therefore accept the existing order and devote ourselves to higher things than politics, to the things of God that transcend this world, to preparation for eternal life."

This attitude, which may have been the best attitude— or at least a defensible one—for Christians in many other circumstances, is not possible for us. A book has just been written on the subject of this lecture by a very able English layman, Walter James, an editor of the *Times* of London.

Its title is *The Christian in Politics*.[1] He tends to play down the importance of the political life, and he emphasizes the fact that Christians have often been indifferent to politics in the past. He says this: "If one believes that through the original revelation, and in the guidance of the church by the Holy Spirit since then, God has given to man all that he needs for salvation, then these difficulties about politics [lack of New Testament guidance, etc.] may be taken perhaps to indicate the relative unimportance of this sphere beside personal living."[2] I agree that it is important to regard politics as subordinate to many of the values realized in personal living; there is no greater political perversion than to turn all questions into political questions. But the whole tendency of Mr. James' book seems to suggest that politics is an optional interest. It may be such an optional interest in a static society in which not much is expected to happen to bring more than usual of either good or evil. But today we confront changes of a fateful nature which promise new possibilities for humanity and threaten us with a hell on earth, and the political choices which we make may help to determine the direction of change. Those choices may have a profound effect on "personal living."

I said that one of the elements in this new situation in which we live is that most human groups can now make themselves heard. This robs us of the moral possibility of complacently accepting an unjust *status quo*. This has not always been the case. The contemporary tendency of Christians to emphasize the claims of a more equal justice goes against the major traditions in the church. On the whole, as Mr. James says: "While it is true that a few Christians in most periods professed egalitarian views, the great majority of them from the beginning to Bishop Gore's own day [the late 19th and early 20th centuries] had

[1]Oxford University Press, 1962.
[2]*Ibid*, p. 37.

regarded a social hierarchy as written in the scheme of things."[1] Mr. James and many others suggest that the contemporary Christian preoccupation with the struggle for greater equality is merely a case of following fashionable trends. Instead it is suggested that the church should look to its earlier wisdom and keep itself free from modern egalitarian movements. There are forms of this quest for equality which are based upon illusions and which should be rejected. But at the heart of the quest for equality there are two things which are valid. One is the emphasis on what we might call equality of consideration for all people regardless of their race or class. The other is the recognition that while there must be functional hierarchies, every particular hierarchical system, when it becomes hardened, is pervaded by injustice. It becomes an embodiment of pride and greed.

To all who say that Christians, if they would only be more sophisticated, more patient, more religious, could avoid political concern, and especially could avoid all preoccupation with the claims of people for equality of consideration, I say this: "While you can find many precedents in Christian history for your position, our predecessors lacked one essential element in our experience; they did not have a chance to listen to the many who were exploited and neglected, who were the victims of dehumanizing indignities and deprivations. Our predecessors performed many acts of charity and did many things to soften the lot of these people; but they seldom had a chance to see the world from their point of view." Indeed it is only now that in the United States the Negro is finding a voice that can speak with utter frankness to the white man, and the white man now knows that he was often self-deceived about the race which he has used for his own purposes and on which he still imposes continuous and organized humiliations.

[1] *The Christian in Politics*, p. 129.

The industrial workers were the first to find this voice of protest, and often they used the language of Marxism. Now around the world we have to listen to the people who formerly were silent and neglected. This new experience has demolished the conservative interpretations of divine providence which caused Christians in other periods to support slavery, absolute monarchy, the squire's superior privilege, the earlier institutions of capitalism, the imperialism that did not plan to make itself dispensable. This new experience has proved the inadequacy of paternalistic interpretations of Christian love that made it seem enough to do good things for people without raising the question of one's power over them or one's superior privilege.

This new experience to which I refer does not mean that we should assume that those to whom we must now listen are right in all of their judgments, or that we should accept their political panaceas. Nor must we assume that when they gain power they will not be tempted to abuse it as much as did the former mighty who have been overthrown. Nor does it mean that we must accept the idea that it is always right to give self-government as soon as there are strong voices that demand it. Indeed, Christians must know that the sins of man are not produced by any economic or social system but that men in all economic and social systems are proud and self-centred and can at times be controlled by hatred and cruelty. Political warnings of this sort are often needed, though perhaps they have been too well learned by white Christians in Europe and North America in this decade. Moral lectures from white men to the people who are just beginning to get power are not very convincing. The reality which is more important for political morality and which Christians after some cleansing shocks should be able to recognize is that comfortable and powerful people can no longer neglect, humiliate or trample upon vast multitudes without full awareness of what they are doing.

I shall now outline very briefly the answer that I give to those who raise the question: What is there that is Christian in any political decision? After it is explained that there is no Christian politics, that there is no Christian government, that there should be no Christian political party, that there is no self-sufficient Christian guidance for political decisions, what then are the Christian ingredients in any political judgments? I shall mention five such ingredients.

The first is that Christians should have the habit of seeing all political communities, systems, policies under the judgment and mercy of God. And this does not mean that we see them under the judgment and mercy of some vague Supreme Being, for it is extremely easy to enlist such a Supreme Being or Almighty on our side, whatever it is. The God to whom we refer is revealed in the Bible. It is dangerous to take odd verses or episodes from the Bible and make these accidentally normative. You can get together a number of such passages to support total war, the annihilation of the enemy, the most vindictive and self-righteous spirit in any conflict. But it is exactly this spirit which has no place in the Christian approach to politics. It is a commonplace of all theological discussion of these issues today that the basic sin in the political sphere is a form of idolatry, the absolutizing of our own culture, social system, nation or party. Usually modern men may not formally turn these objects of loyalty into gods but instead claim for them the full support of the God in whom they believe or half-believe. They are quite incapable of understanding what Amos did when he moved from the judgment upon Damascus, Gaza, Tyre, Edom, the Ammonites, Moab, Judah to Israel saying:

> For three transgressions of Israel,
>   and for four, I will not revoke the Punishment,
>   because they sell the righteous for silver and
>   the needy for a pair of shoes.

and they are less capable of understanding the main point that Amos makes when he says:

> You only have I known of all the families of the earth;
> Therefore I will punish you for all your iniquities.

We could debate the question: Is there much chance for citizens of a nation or those who are the children of a particular culture to avoid for long making idols out of the ideals and the systems and communities which they prize if they have no transcendent source of jugment upon all things human? Certainly individuals can do this, and there may be a relativism shared by many sophisticated people which is beneficent in so far as it prevents this kind of idolatry. But such relativism is likely to be debilitating, and it is likely to leave a vacuum that is easily filled by crude idolatries. Reinhold Niebuhr likes to say that Abraham Lincoln was one of the greatest American theologians though only a few of his pages can be called theological. As a statesman he understood this central point about the danger of idolatry, for he saw both sides in the great struggle in which he was involved under the same God and he resolutely refused to identify either side, even his own, in an absolute way with the divine will. Today in the cold war many of us in the west are tempted to see the conflict in simple terms as a struggle between those who worship God and atheists. But this turns advocates of the western cause into idolaters. If there is one thing that the churches should say to the people of North America, it is that this cold war is no holy war. We must not add the fury of a religious crusade to this very serious conflict between the nations in which vital political and moral issues are at stake.[1]

The second element in Christian thinking and deciding about political problems can be understood as an extension

[1]Pope John's encyclical, *Pacem in Terris*, gives strong support to those who oppose the idea of a holy war against Communism.

of the first: it is response to the love of God for all men, not
a passive benevolence but an outgoing love for the whole
world which was demonstrated in the incarnation, in God's
coming in Christ into our history. Already I have said some
of the things that are involved here, and have presupposed
the way in which Christ himself concentrated on the people
of greatest need, the people whom respectable society
neglected or despised. It is this aggressive caring for the
marginal people who cannot defend themselves which is
essential when the Christian makes political judgments.
This has to do with the attitude that society takes toward
delinquents and criminals. There can be no place for
punishments based upon vindictive rejection of the criminal;
no place, I should say, for capital punishment. I do not mean
that there are no emergencies in which the state may not
take life. Karl Barth says that while capital punishment
should have no place in the regular processes of government,
there may be crises in which some forms of treason against
the very existence of society call for the death penalty.
About this I am not sure, for shooting alleged traitors is
often much too tempting. Barth cannot make a judgment
that would rule out tyrannicide in the case of Hitler. With
this I have more sympathy.[1]

One of the most important implications of the Christian
response to the love of God for all men is the command of
Jesus that we love our enemies. This command is never
repealed by the demands of any conflict or emergency. We
need not derive pacifist conclusions from this command,
but whatever be the tragic circumstances in which one
human group is at war with another human group, it must
never be forgotten that the enemies are human, loved of
God, a part of the world which Christ came to save, and our
responsibility for them remains.

The third element in the guidance that Christians bring

[1]*Church Dogmatics*, III, 4, pp. 437-450.

to politics is an understanding of human nature that is in some respects unique. I shall mention two aspects of this view of man. In both cases I shall refer to a balance in the Christian view that is often in practice obscured. One aspect is the way in which Christian theology sees all men as made in the image of God and at the same time emphasizes the depth and universality of sin, the pride and self-centredness of all human groups. There is warning here against cynicism and dogmatic pessimism and against sentimentalism and utopianism. Christian thought is at this point different from many rationalistic or idealistic forms of democratic thinking, different also from Marxist thinking which presupposes an ultimate solution of the human problem through the transformation of economic institutions. The most important effect on the behaviour of nations and other large scale groups of the Christian understanding of the pervasiveness of sin is for all of us who grasp its significance to apply it to ourselves as an antidote to self-righteousness. Reinhold Niebuhr, Herbert Butterfield and other thinkers have helped our generation to see that the self-righteous blindness or fury of nations is the most destructive force in recent history.

The other element in the Christian view of man that has great relevance to contemporary political controversies is the precise way in which man is seen both as an individual person, responsible for his own commitments and decisions, and as a member of the community. Christian theology provides a radical criticism of stereotypes of both individualism and collectivism. My fellow citizens south of the border who follow Senator Goldwater—or those to the right of him who form the incredible John Birch Society—and the Communists should both feel aware of a conflict between their political philosophy and Christianity. Unfortunately, the former do not usually feel that conflict but wrap themselves in a Christian garment.

A fourth Christian factor in political life may not be so much an element in our political judgments as it is a resource for living with our political judgments. It is the mediation of grace and forgiveness to those who are aware of their sharing in the corporate sin that is always present in political life. Instead of escaping from all of the more morally ambiguous spheres of activity, and instead of being unnerved by guilt or despair, Christians know the experience of receiving grace and forgiveness while they take responsibility. Emil Brunner has put the matter very accurately, though in what may be forbidding theological language, in these words: "We never see the real meaning of 'original sin', we never perceive the depth and universality of evil, or what evil means in the depths common to us all, until we are *obliged* to do something in our official capacity— for the sake of order, and therefore the sake of love—which apart from our 'office', would be absolutely wrong."[1] Anyone working on the designing, the manufacture, or the placing of nuclear weapons, and anyone who votes to acquire them for the nation's defence, must feel the force of this statement. It is possible to form the judgment that your nation or mine should have nothing to do with this preparation for nuclear war, but if we make that decision we are deciding that there is to be no way of checking the misuse of nuclear power by another nation. The problem arises, of course, before we get to nuclear weapons in any preparation to use lethal weapons. All that I maintain here is that even that choice makes one responsible for other evils which one has decided not to take relevant measures to prevent. There is no escape from involvement in evil for pacifist or non-pacifist.

The whole world of power and of actual and potential violence is the most obvious sphere of the evil in political life, but all political decisions must be based upon a consensus

[1] *The Divine Imperative* (Lutterworth, 1937), p. 227.

which presupposes compromises and accommodations that trouble the conscience and tempt one to withdraw to the compromises of private life. In Protestant circles in the United States there is a tendency to exaggerate the corruption of politics assuming business to be morally clean, but it is forgotten that the corruption of politics usually comes from the pressure of business interests upon politicians.

In recent decades Protestant theology has had an answer to those who realize that this is a sinful world in which most of our political decisions are at least the source of conflicts of conscience. The answer given to Christians who found themselves in this kind of moral perplexity was, "Take responsibility for the lesser evil and live under the grace and mercy of God." One of the favourite phrases that gained currency in this context was Luther's injunction, "Sin bravely," and this was taken to mean, "Be resolute and faithful to your responsibility for order and justice even when you become involved in evils which torment your conscience."

I believe that this kind of political realism is a most important contribution of Christian faith to responsible living in the world as it is. It is an alternative to various forms of escape—escape into monastic or separatist communities, or escape into idealistic exhortations which are irrelevant to available political alternatives.

Without taking back anything that I have said about Christian political realism, I want to say now that this political realism has itself often become too rigid. It has often become a position that is no longer under Christian criticism. It often becomes a rationalization of whatever seems necessary for western strategy in the cold war. One of my chief interests at present is to try to bring this political realism, which has gained too much momentum of its own under the pressure of events, back under Christian criticism.

The fifth Christian resource for political decision and

action may surprise you. In some ways it is not so much another resource as the mediator of the four Christian resources which I have mentioned. I refer to the presence in all of our communities of the church. Some of you may think of the church as nothing more than the buildings which are familiar landmarks in your communities. The mention of them may make you yawn. They may seem little more than the conventional furniture of Canadian or American culture. Above all, they may seem irrelevant to the great political issues which trouble us. I can agree with almost every particular criticism of churches as we know them, but I shall call attention to several aspects of the church which often go unnoticed.

1.   Is it not a surprising fact that in almost every city, town and village of Canada and the United States there are these institutions or communities called churches which are under no local or national authority, which have their origin in events nearly two thousand years ago in a distant land, which have their charter in a book that came from a very different culture? This church has a real independence of both nation and state. Even in those countries where there is a traditional established church, the church is required by its very nature to seek freedom from the control of the state in its own inner life at the least, and it also often finds itself struggling for freedom to witness to divine judgment on the institutions and policies of the state. It may fail to secure this latter freedom, it may not even miss that kind of freedom very much, and yet there are in the church's tradition reminders of its responsibility to take freedom to obey God rather than men in public life.

2.   The church is present in nearly every country of the world. Not only that; it has been able to form a universal Christian community (technically it is not a universal church because of its own divisons), and this universal Christian

community is becoming more and more real to its members in the various countries. This is quite a recent development. Today we can say that more than at any time since the Reformation, Roman Catholics, Protestants and Orthodox are aware of belonging together to this universal Christian community if not to the same empirical church.

3. The church has a surprising way of rising to occasions. Often its spiritual condition is best when it is in material distress or under attack from the principalities and powers in the world. This cannot be guaranteed, but it is a common enough occurrence to receive emphasis. If secular communities or institutions break down, the chance is quite good that the church will receive new life. This is not a reason for the church to encourage a secular catastrophe! One of the great episodes of modern church history was the resistance of an important part of the German church to Hitler. There was much that was glorious and also socially creative in that episode. A good case can be made for the view that if the German church had had better preparation in relating Christianity to politics, it would have been able to act much sooner and would have had a greater political effect in the 1920's and early 1930's. One of the pillars of the German Confessing Church which did resist Hitler, the late Professor Iwand of Bonn University, said, "If the evangelical churches of Germany had been clearer in their own thinking about what a state could and could not do and what a Christian could and could not permit, the assumption of power by National Socialism would have been more effectively resisted."[1] I may add that in addition to a more relevant theology and ethics, there would have had to be more political sophistication than was present in the church. This suggests what is possible if the church does gain political

[1]Quoted by Amos Wilder in *The Background of the New Testament and Its Eschatology*, edited by Davies & Danbe (Cambridge University Press, 1956), p. 522.

awareness. Even in the Communist countries, where the churches have been so much controlled by the regimes that they have been subject to severe criticism in the west for their docility, it now seems that they have considerable vitality and that they are the only large-scale non-political institutions which have been able to preserve some independence of the state in their inner life. The church has been proved to have a surprising toughness.

4. The church stands for the human over against all systems and ideologies. This is one of the chief emphases of Karl Barth, and we can all appropriate it. Where there is a tendency to see all persons in political terms, as political instruments to be used for a political cause, as opponents to be pushed aside or liquidated, or as candidates for nuclear annihilation, the church by its worship and its witness and pastoral service keeps reminding a nation that man transcends all of these schemes and these forms of partisanship and enmity in his ultimate relationship, in his meaning and his destiny. One example of this role of the church is that Christians who are citizens of nations that have conflicting interests and may be adversaries in bitter conflicts are also members of this universal community. It has been my privilege in recent months to spend some days with churchmen behind the Iron Curtain and many weeks with churchmen in Asia, and I have a very vivid sense of this common membership in the Christian community as prior to the many different interests and commitments which we have as citizens of our nations. But there is something more. I do not believe that this means that all Christians should think of themselves as belonging to a Christian community that seeks special consideration for its members over against other communities of men. On the contrary, Christians represent to each other the feelings, the needs and aspirations and anxieties of non-Christian neighbours. This is another example of the way in which the church represents

the human. Because of our relationship with Christians in other countries, we cannot think of the people of those other countries primarily in political terms. I, for example, must not see them primarily in their relation to American interests or policy.

5.   A final aspect of the church is that if one sees it over a long enough period, or over a wide enough area, one finds a tendency for it to be renewed and reformed. Protestants have often assumed that because it is a part of the very structure of their churches that they always stand under the judgment of God's Word which they confront as an *other* which they cannot control, they can expect this periodic renewal. Today Protestants may be surprised to find themselves inspired by the ferment in the Roman Catholic Church. If you thought that you could write off the Roman Church as in the grip of an authoritarian system that was incapable of self-criticism, you now know that this was a miscalculation. Indeed, the Catholics are probably surprising themselves at the present time. They hear cardinals say publicly what the bolder spirits used to say privately. This new ferment in the Roman Church may have very beneficial political consequences in many countries. I have in mind how it may affect in quite different ways developments in North and South America. There are many examples of the renewal of the Protestant churches, but they are less centralized and less publicized.

The familiar Christian idea of dual citizenship in two cities, the histories of which are intermingled in many ways as St. Augustine saw so clearly, has momentous consequences for the political order of the earthly city. There is a parallel to this conception in the experience of contemporary scientists. When scientists from both sides of the Iron Curtain meet, they have an experience of a similar dual citizenship though they would be careful to avoid putting it in that way. They can communicate with each other far better in their own field than can the politicians. They realize that they are open to realities which the political powers cannot control. They can even reach tentative agreements on disarmament that may escape the political negotiators. Christians who participate in this dual citizenship are constrained to realize the limits of the earthly political city; in giving signs of these limits, whether they know it or not, they open the door to the freedom of all citizens to give similar signs of their transcendence of that city. They continually call nation and state to be open to God's judgment and love and to the humanity of all men.

II

THE CONFLICT OF IDEOLOGIES
IN THE COLD WAR

In this lecture I shall deal with the great conflict between ideologies that divides the world so deeply and that makes all other conflicts so much more dangerous and more difficult to overcome. I realize that in Canada there is at least a shade of difference in the way this conflict appears as compared with the United States. Here the words "China" and "Cuba" have a different effect on the blood pressure than is the case with us. In order to be fully fair to the United States you would have to imagine Florida as a province of Canada. Geography does make a difference. Also, you probably realize that American power, which in some respects is an embarrassment to us and an annoyance to you, makes us the only nation that can provide a check on the power in the Communist bloc. This power has created a responsibility, and it also makes the United States the most obvious target for Communist hostility. The result has been to drive us in the United States into an excessive preoccupation with Communism. You may regret this, but you should understand it.

There is an additional factor in the American situation that creates a special intransigence in some circles. This is the presence of an extreme economic conservatism that cannot distinguish between Communism, socialism and the very modest institutions of the welfare state that we have in the United States. These conservatives are in a panic because this failure to make any distinctions whenever they look to the left of themselves causes them to feel surrounded by an ocean of Communism with the tide coming in. They lash out against the most innocent targets and they create much confusion. Fortunately they do not run the government, and on a show-down they can command many more dollars than votes.

I shall first emphasize the distinction between the conflict of faith between Christianity and Communism on the one hand and the political conflict between the nations on the other. There are vital issues at stake in the international conflict, more vital issues than Karl Barth, the greatest Protestant theologian, thinks, for example. In 1949 he said of the conflict between Russia and America: "As Christians it is not our concern at all. It is not a genuine, not a necessary, not an interesting conflict. It is a mere power conflict."[1] It may do many of us good to hear that, but it is surely an overstatement of a correction. More recently Barth made light of the conflict in his famous letter to a pastor in East Germany. In that letter he seemed to equate the dangers from both sides with a plague-on-both-your-houses neutralism and likened the American way of life to the flesh-pots of Egypt.[2] (Recently when he was in New York he was asked at a press conference about that statement. He replied, in a most characteristic way, "There are many good things to say about Egypt.") Later I shall say more about what is at stake in the conflict between the nations. I must now say that we should distinguish between that conflict and the very profound struggle between Christianity and Communism for the minds and souls of men.

This spiritual struggle goes on within the Communist nations themselves, for Christians there continue to resist the Communist ideology. They fight against atheism and against the Marxist understanding of man and history. In this struggle they do not want to be considered political allies of the west. Often their leaders join in the political

[1] *Against the Stream* (S.C.M. Press, 1954), p. 131.
[2] *How to Serve God in a Marxist Land* (Association Press, 1959), p. 69.

propaganda of their governments against the west. I believe that this has caused most of us in western countries to be unfair to them and to discount their important achievement in preserving Christian enclaves in what is intended to be a Marxist culture. It is only recently that many of us have been made aware of the extent of this achievement, especially in the Soviet Union. The church in Russia, with twenty-five million or more active believers, is more vital than anyone could have expected. As the ideological fanaticism is eroded, the church will be there to take advantage of new opportunities. We in the western nations must realize that on the other side of the Iron Curtain the spiritual struggle continues to go on. It is not a struggle for a political victory for the west, and we should not seek to take advantage of it in those terms. It is a struggle for religious freedom, for Christian faith, and for a more humane society in the Communist world.

There are two reasons for avoiding in our circles the identification of this Christian conflict with Communism with the international conflict. The first is the obvious one that when we combine the passions of religion with the passions of politics we get the worst of both. The result is a kind of holy war which makes impossible the political accommodations and compromises on which the fragile life of humanity depends. In a holy war you are likely to insist on the enemy's unconditional surrender. It may help us to remember that the official atheism of Communism, tragic as it is in its human consequences, is itself in large part the result of the failure of Christians. If the churches had understood fifty years ago what the capitalistic industrialism of that time was doing to people and had taken the part of its victims, it is quite possible that the political and social conflicts of our period would not have the religious dimension which creates so deep a split in humanity.

A second reason for avoiding the identification of these two conflicts is that while the present international conflict tends to separate people, so that Christians have difficulty across international lines in meeting Communists as persons, the religious confrontation of Christianity and Communism calls for relationships, for love rather than hostility, for persuasion rather than nuclear threats. It is well to remember that in some countries Christians and Communists still have opportunities to meet as persons. Adlai Stevenson a few years ago said, "I recall the anti-Communist youth delegation that called on me in France and left a friend outside in the car because he was a Communist."[1] It is also important to remember that completely dedicated Communists are a small minority in all the Communist countries. If Christians wage a holy war against nations, they cut themselves off not only from Communists as persons but also from large populations which, if they could be reached, would be more open to the Christian message.

Christians who have been influenced by the ecumenical movements, by the World Council of Churches and ecumenical student movements, have avoided the holy war psychology. For this reason these ecumenical institutions are under bitter attack in some circles in the United States. One of the most encouraging developments in this context is the change of attitude in the Roman Catholic Church. There has always been a difference between the Vatican and European Catholicism (outside of Spain) and American Catholicism on this issue. American Catholics have often combined a religious hostility to Communism with super-patriotism. But the Vatican has moved under Pope John to a more open attitude toward Communist nations, and in the United States there is a decline of the fanatical anti-Communism that was very common in

[1] *Call to Greatness* (Harper, 1954), p. 31.

Catholic circles a few years ago. McCarthyism was in large measure a Catholic phenomenon, partly a tribal Irish phenomenon. But the Catholic Church has given no official support to the present rightist movements in the states. Unfortunately these seem to be a Protestant phenomenon, flourishing chiefly in a few regions where there is much extreme Fundamentalism but always opposed to the national leaders of Protestantism.

I began by making a distinction between the religious conflict between Christianity and Communism and the international conflict between west and east. I want now to make another distinction that will control much of what I have to say in this lecture. This is the distinction between Communism as a faith, a system of thought, and a movement of committed people controlled by that faith and thought, and Communist nations which are influenced not only by ideology but by their historical experience, by nationalism and by the passing of generations. Communism is not one entity that can be adequately understood by reading the texts of Marx and Lenin. Indeed, the very establishment of Communist regimes in countries that had not gone very far in industrial development was a break with Marx's own expectations. Today we have to do with a spectrum of Communist nations which runs from China on the left to Poland and Yugoslavia on the right, with the Soviet Union in the centre. If we are to deal wisely with the reality of Communism, we must make this distinction.

This does not mean that it is unimportant to consider Communism as a faith and an ideological system that has possessed the minds and souls of millions of people in our time. Communism in this sense may be strongest among those who are in the early stages of revolutionary struggle. Another consideration is that not only convinced Communists but also much of the population in the Soviet Union and other Communist countries inevitably see the world through ideological lenses. Even if they have lost the revolutionary fanaticism of an earlier period, there may remain considerable rigidity of thought. The strong prejudice against all religion will remain as part of the culture. No one can be sure how to measure the degree of Communist aggressiveness which remains even though it may be on the decline. Western statesmen who are well aware of the changes that have taken place in the Soviet Union and of the diversities in the Communist world are rightly cautious in drawing conclusions from these developments concerning the foreign policy of the Soviet Union.

What is the basic issue between Communism as a system and Christianity? I do not believe that we should look for the most important sources of conflict to Communism as an economic system, or to Communism as involving revolution, even violent revolution. Nor should we emphasize as central the fact of dictatorship, which is in theory expected to be transitional. Whatever we do, we must not think of putting capitalism or a free enterprise system over against Communism and defending it in Christian terms. I should not start even with the atheism of Communism. As I shall suggest in a moment, this constitutes a serious problem as it becomes hardened, but atheist rebellion against caricatures of God can be a sign of health.

Rather we should locate the centre of the conflict in the fact that Communism tends to be a closed system of commitment and thought that makes absolute claims. It claims to be the true philosophy, the true theory of religion, the true explanation of history, the true programme for social development, the one hope for man as a social being. This absolute system exists in many minds, and for a time it has become embodied in the institutions of nations. Even when it has been modified, the sense of absoluteness has often accompanied the modifications. The changes that come over it that have most hope in them are not those that are designed and then rationalized by a manipulation of the doctrine, but rather those that are the result of a less conscious process of mixing Communism with nationalism or of the dilutions which come when revolutionaries are succeeded by scientists, technicians and builders.

When Christians confront this absolute system, they must oppose it by personal witness and by the teaching of the church. And when they find that Communists seek to impose this sytem on others by force, by threats, by the wiles of political manipulators and conspirators, Christians have a responsibility to work politically to counteract these activities, even to the extent of preserving military power in the non-Communist world to offset the military power of Communist nations. In detail there are many things to argue about here, especially about the occasions on which military power should be used, but in the main I believe that the case on Christian grounds for this kind of opposition to Communism can be well defended.

I have spoken in general terms about Communism as an absolute system. I think that we should emphasize three aspects of that system.

First, there is no God above it, no ultimate source of judgment or mercy beyond society. Intellectual atheism as a form of rebellion against false conceptions of God is not in itself the most important problem for Christians in Communism, but it does rob those who are trained as Communists of the chance to be open to God's revelation. We may see in Communist absolutism a kind of idolatry, for it puts the Communist scheme or the ultimate Communist society in place of God and then protects and hardens this idolatry by means of theoretical atheism.

Secondly, one of the outcroppings of Communist absolutism is the belief that when the revolution has reached its goal it will overcome the social evils from which humanity has always suffered. One mark of this expectation is the belief that there will be no more need of the state as a coercive force in society. Communism, in common with many modern philosophies, has no understanding of the deep sources of evil in man. It assumes that the eradication of the institutions of capitalism will remove the causes of injustice, oppression and war. I have had occasion to speak of this aspect of Communism for many years, but today it is so obviously false that I hardly have the patience to expound it. Until recently, all of the internal unsolved problems in Communist countries might be explained as belonging to a transitional stage in the dialectical process. But the rift between the two great Communist nations must cause even faithful Communists to wonder if they have in their control the means of putting an end to large-scale social conflict. The difference between Christianity and Communism that will be most quickly tested is this difference in the understanding of man and the perennial sources of his pride, his egoism and his will to power. Communism's promise of a fully rational society if only it achieves political power is probably the chief source of its most repellent features. It provides the motive and the excuse to use all possible means to win power and to impose the Communist will upon a nation. Revolutionary violence is so common that it cannot be associated with Communism in a special way, but rationalized terror by a totalitarian state in controlling a people and a culture can be attributed to Communism, and it may be supported for decades by the belief that the Communist party represents the good future of humanity.

Thirdly, Christians must reject Communism as a system for its failure to provide an adequate place for the individual person, for the independent mind and spirit, for the person's own search for truth, for the conscience that is not under political guidance. The current intellectual ferment in the Soviet Union indicates that this is the aspect of Communism that is now widely rejected. One of the most reassuring facts about Russian society is that decades of education, censorship, propaganda and terror have not succeeded in destroying the inner longings for truth transcending the will of the party or the state. Communism may be too optimistic about future society, but out of the struggles of our period we have learned something from the failures of Communism: we have learned that there is a good toughness in the human spirit that often preserves it from dehumanization. Christians may understand this as a mark of the divine image in man or of what Calvinists call "common grace"— the sustaining grace of God that is present in civil society even outside the Christian circle, even among atheists.[1]

Against the background of this Communist neglect of the person, one can see the clearest moral conflict between Communism and Christianity. There is no dimension in Communism that makes it possible to say that we must never treat an individual person only as a political obstacle to be removed. From the Christian standpoint every person has status because God loves him even if party and state reject him. Christians can never be satisfied to change the institutions of society and scrap concrete persons for the sake of the future of society. There is something hollow about my saying this when non-Communist nations influenced by Christianity can contemplate as readily as they do the incineration of large populations in nuclear war for the sake of political objectives. This is a complicated matter, and the best thing that we can say is that such action can never be finally rationalized in Christian terms, as totalitarian

[1]It is impossible to keep up with the rapid changes in the Soviet Union in regard to artistic freedom. At the moment the authorities are curbing the artists and writers, but these are not victims of Stalin's type of terror. The conflict is out in the open and the intellectual ferment is a serious problem for the authorities. To some extent there seems to be a conflict between generations. There are signs of deep conflict in the Soviet Union and the future is precarious. It will be difficult to re-create the monolith either in the Soviet Union or in the Communist world as a whole.

terror has been rationalized in Communist terms. Again what I say may seem hollow because Christians do sometimes rationalize it. I seem to be saying that Christians in war have perpetrated and prepare to perpetrate acts of violence that exceed in cruel destructiveness anything yet done by Communists but that in their hearts they know that they are under judgment and that when they use violence they are indeed very sorry that there are so many victims and that they cannot wait to send the survivors aid and to help them to rebuild their nations. Something like that is what I am saying, and it reveals our moral predicament. It might be well to reflect that next time, after a nuclear war, there are not likely to be the resources for another Marshall Plan. But this is really an aside.

Now I shall go back to my distinction between Communism as an ideological system and the various Communist nations. One of the chief reasons for hope that we may be able to live with these nations and that something may come out of Communism in some of them that is better than critics of Communism have expected is that great changes have taken place in Russia since the death of Stalin and several of the eastern European nations are diluting Communism by combining it with national cultures. The leaders of these countries are not going to announce that they have abandoned the ideology or objectives of Communism, but there can develop a change in priorities, and new impulses not allowed for in the dialectic can modify the purposes of the society. Russian education had been assumed to be no more than indoctrination, but it seems to have stimulated many people to think for themselves at least in non-political spheres. The desire for peace as an independent goal and not as a by-product of the victory of Communism is clearly a powerful force among the people, and it influences national policy. The desire for consumer goods, for a bourgeois standard of living, for opportunities for private life, certainly undercuts ideological fanaticism. Such changes as these call for changed attitudes toward Communist nations. Perhaps the clearest change is in the attitude toward war. Khrushchev made the following statement, the clearest that I have seen: "As Marxist-Leninists, we cannot conceive the creation of a Communist civilization on the ruins of the world's cultural centres, upon a world deserted and poisoned by thermonuclear fall-out."[1] The only thing wrong with that statement is that is has nothing to do with Marxist-Leninism.

As I have said, the tendency in the United States is for the government, while it is fully aware of these changes, to wait to be shown before it takes a very hopeful view of Soviet foreign policy. There is also fear that premature optimism would lead to a popular relaxation. Official caution along these lines is probably justified. But a sense of the gradations of Communism should on a deeper level than policy cause us to overcome the black-and-white view of the world that has been so natural to us since about 1947. Our absolute hostility toward the Communist world as an irreformable slave world should erode to match the erosion of Communist absolutism. Co-existence may then become a reality marked by co-operation as well as by competition. The foolish talk of total victory in the cold war should cease. There will be new and unexpected problems and there will be new fears, but with the disappearance of the nightmare of having to choose between a Stalinist slave world and nuclear annihilation it may be possible to think in more human terms even about the issues of world politics.

What should Christians stand for in the present ideological conflict? Let us try to get behind the obvious stereotypes and slogans to consider the political criteria and goals that

[1]Speech in Berlin, Jan. 1963, quoted in *Newsweek*, Jan. 28, 1963, p. 44.

should guide Christians in our countries, not only as good for ourselves but as good for all nations. I am not suggesting that all nations should model their institutions after ours or that our form of democracy should be exported everywhere but that there may be principles of political life that Christians in all countries might hope to see embodied in their national institutions. Before I have completed my exposition you may see that I try to allow for the great variety of historical limitations and possibilities and yet to avoid a complete moral and political relativism. I believe that there are three political criteria or objectives that are important everywhere though they are not perfectly realized anywhere and though different countries will have to find their own different ways of combining them.

The first is the idea of the limited state, the state limited by law and by the existence of institutions within the nation which represent non-political interests. One of these non-political institutions is, of course, the church or other religious bodies. Spiritual and cultural freedom depends always upon two things acting upon each other. One is the development of legal limits on the state. The other is the development within the nation of institutions and groups that keep pressing for freedom. Even in the Soviet Union, according to our authorities on the Soviet legal system, there has been in the post-Stalinist era an encouraging development of legal restraints upon governments. At the same time there is a circle of artists and other intellectuals who take some freedom, encountering rebuffs but succeeding within narrow limits in expressing themselves. I mention the Soviet Union not because it is a good example of the limited state but because it is one of the last places where one would expect to find this development.

The second criterion or objective is a state that is committed to the promotion of social justice and welfare for the whole population. This is platitudinous enough, but it may be one of the providential aspects of Communism that it has forced the authorities in many nations for the first time to take it seriously. It took the threat of Castroism to cause the United States to realize the need of revolutionary change in most Latin American countries. Communism as a scourge has forced nations to put social justice and welfare much higher on the agenda than they would otherwise have done. Churches have been aroused by this challenge. I learned recently that a conference in Brazil under the auspices of the Protestant churches has used as its slogan, "Christ the Lord of the Latin American Revolution." This is a new note among Protestants in Latin America. There are also new voices of a similar kind in the Roman Catholic Church in Latin America.

The third criterion or objective is participation in political life by all parts of the population, with no racial or social group deprived of the suffrage. I put this last because I want to avoid the tendency to assume that universal suffrage is a panacea for everything. Also, I think that we must accept the fact that many governments for a long time will be more authoritarian than we would permit ours to be. On the other hand, in the long run the movement toward participation in political life by the whole population is of enormous importance if most of the people are not to be exploited or neglected by those who have the power. In the United States we have learned this only too well from the experience of the Negro minority in those states where they have been denied the vote by law or by administrative subterfuge. In those states the Negroes have had the worst of everything, and the politicians have often been racial demagogues. A change in Negro voting rights will at least mean a change of politicians and give the minority some power to defend itself. (Already one of the chief instruments of racial justice is the balance of political power held by Negroes in important northern states.) I do not mean to play down this aspect of democracy in putting it last, but we should not separate it from the first criterion involving limited government. Majority rule by the ballot is no safeguard against tyranny unless there are legal protections for minorities.

These three criteria or objectives taken together are equivalent to what we mean in our two countries by democracy. In the long run all three are interdependent. Important as limited government is, it is no substitute for government that is effective in meeting social needs. If government fails for too long in meeting those needs, the way may be prepared for totalitarian movements that work for an unlimited state. A government that is not responsible to the people as a whole is likely to be unjust and to serve the interests of whatever clique has the power. But popular government without legal restraints is likely to become a tyranny, perhaps beginning as a tyranny of those who speak for the majority. In the present ideological conflict, therefore, we should work for an open world in which with varying patterns all countries will be encouraged to move toward these three objectives.

Without in any way taking back what I have said about the universal relevance of these objectives, I believe that it is important for us to show tolerance toward many of the political and economic experiments of other nations. We must recognize that at times the primary need may be a government that is strong enough to govern; at other times, social and economic revolution. Some experts whom I trust say that in several Latin American countries the dynamism favourable to necessary social changes is to be found chiefly in movements that use Marxist language. These may not be Communist, and they need not be agents of the Soviet Union or of China. There is a possibility that for several countries a somewhat loose national Marxism may be the best available alternative in the near future. I fear that in the United States there may be intolerance of such a loose national Marxism and that the countries involved may be pushed into Communism of the kind that would be more of a threat to the hemisphere. I hope that the United States can learn to be tolerant enough to prevent this from happening. It is one of our American problems that while the national administration is often flexible about matters of this kind, as it has been with regard to aid to Yugoslavia and Poland, Congress is still inclined toward a destructive rigidity in relation to anyone who uses Marxist language.

What has Christian ethics to do with all that I have said about this democratic pattern of political life? Here I can only refer back to two parts of my first lecture. It is true that most forms of Christianity in the past have assumed a more hierarchical structure of society than would be compatible with democracy, but the churches and Christians have been shaken by modern events, and have had the opportunity to see the world much more vividly from the point of view of the races and classes that until recently had neither the voice nor the power to call attention to their needs. Also, let me remind you of three of the five Christian contributions to political life that I outlined: the transcendence of God above all earthly powers, the love of God for all men and the balanced understanding of human nature. These three contributions, if they are taken together, constitute strong spiritual support for democratic institutions. Any one of them by itself is not necessarily favourable to democracy. There can be a belief in God's transcendence in the context of an oppressive theocracy ruled by a church or an oligarchy of Christians convinced that they and they alone know the will of God. Emphasis on the love of God for all men, taken by itself, may lead only to a paternalistic serving of those who are weak and disadvantaged without raising any questions about the disparity of power between those who are served and those who serve, and without any concern about political structures. There can also be a one-sided emphasis on one element in Christian teaching about man, for example the universality of sin, which causes the privileged Christian to decide that any change would probably be for the worse, especially any change which involves the sharing of power between his favoured class and "the people" whom he may fear as a "great beast." One of the great difficulties that we have in relating Christianity to political issues is that an ancient religious tradition has so many facets that it is very easy for one facet to be emphasized in such a way as to produce a great distortion. Only when all three of these contributions of Christian faith to political life are seen in their inter-dependence can Christianity become a source of inspiration and guidance for democracy.

Though I have been speaking of the current ideological conflict I have omitted one of the most important symbols used by the Communists, the symbol of capitalism. I have omitted it because the word has ceased to have any clear meaning. Capitalism as a combination of institutions that are in a continuous process of transformation and not as a system based upon a dogmatic individualistic ideology has served many countries well. But from the Christian point of view there is nothing ultimate or universal in any one economic pattern. The needs of different countries call for economic systems with different ingredients. Some will require much more public initiative in economic life than is thought necessary in the United States or Canada. The new nations, which must solve in decades problems which we have solved gradually over a period of generations with great natural advantages, will need to have a great deal of socialism in their economies. Capitalism also has advantages, however, that should not be excluded by a dogmatic socialism. It provides many centres of initiative and **power** that can make for a healthy pluralism. It takes seriously problems of incentive that a consistent collectivism is not likely to solve. With its market mechanism it provides guidance for production that a system of total planning lacks. The task of most nations will be to find by open experiment the best combination of private and public activities in their economies and to abandon the tendency to deal with these matters by means of slogans and dogmatic ideologies.

I think that the United States is more handicapped by individualistic dogmas than Canada. Even though in the past half-century it has moved far in the direction of a welfare state and has come to recognize that the national community working through government has ultimate responsibility for economic growth and stability, there remains a very strong inhibition against public initiative in many areas where it is necessary. The state does many things and is usually left with responsibility when private institutions fail. In such matters as the renewal of our cities and even provision of adequate schools, housing and medical care, however, there is just enough ingrained individualism that distrusts all action by the state to prevent the adoption of policies bold enough to meet national needs. The United States would benefit from having in its tradition more of a socialist impulse to correct the dominant individualism. I fail to see why debilitating inhibitions should lead us to discount in advance the capacity of the community as a whole to solve directly problems that private enterprise shows no signs of being able to solve.

I want to call your attention to a discussion of these issues by the churches that belong to The World Council of Churches under the heading, "The Responsible Society." This concept has been made the over-all criterion for political order and social justice. It has been developed over a period of about seventeen years of corporate thinking and has been given expression by the Assemblies of the World Council of Churches at Amsterdam, Evanston and New Delhi. While the word "democracy" is not used because it is too ambiguous for world-wide use, the elements of democracy which I have emphasized in this lecture are all involved in this concept of "the responsible society." On the relationship between public and private initiative and controls, this ecumenical teaching is also along the lines of my comments here. Here are a few sentences from the report of the Third Section of the Evanston Assembly in 1954:

> While the state is sometimes the enemy of freedom, under many circumstances the state is the only instrument which can make freedom possible for large sectors of the population. The state is not the source of social justice, but it must be its guardian, ready if necessary to accept responsibility to counteract depression or inflation, to relieve the impact of unemployment, industrial injury, low wages, and unfavorable working conditions, sickness and old age. But in doing so the state remains the servant and not the lord of social justice. Therefore we must warn against the danger that the union of political and economic power may result in an all-controlling state.

I refer to this ecumenical use of the concept of the responsible society for its own sake but also because I find a very great similarity between what is said here and the encyclicals of the popes, especially the recent encyclical of Pope John, *Mater et Magistra*. There is in both sets of documents common Christian guidance that has relevance to the problems of most countries. This guidance transcends the dogmas of both sides in the ideological conflict about economic institutions and practices. It does not tell business men or labour leaders how to deal with their affairs, but it provides a frame of reference that is needed today to correct the aberrations of both right and left.

My final word comes out of an experience that I had in January, 1962, in Czechoslovakia. I was present at a meeting of churchmen from both sides of the Iron Curtain. It was a quiet, unpublicized meeting, quite unlike the big peace conferences, and as a result there was remarkable frankness on both sides. There was one occasion on which the group came very close together in its thinking about society. This was when we discussed some of the problems in industrial society on both sides of the curtain. We came to realize that under different systems there were in fact many of the same problems, such problems as the relation of the individual to big organization, the development of incentive for efficient activity, how to preserve flexibility in a bureaucracy, when to centralize or decentralize activities and controls. We discussed the secularization that is common to our two kinds of society. Obviously there are distinctive difficulties when secularization is promoted by an atheistic state, but it may still be very pervasive when it comes as the unintended by-product of cultural changes. Awareness of such common problems may help to restore communication across the ideological chasm that still divides us.

III

CHRISTIAN ETHICS
AND THE NUCLEAR DILEMMA

I shall begin this lecture with an explanation of the purpose of the kind of thinking about the nuclear dilemma that I want to present to you. I am not an absolutist. I often wish that I were, for thinking, if not living, would be simpler. I can offer no formula that would suggest an immediate escape from the nuclear dilemma. And yet I find it necessary to challenge many of the assumptions that now surround the possession of nuclear armaments and the possibility of nuclear war. There is a reasonably good chance that there will be time to revise some of these assumptions. I speak in the light of that hope. I believe that the churches should use this time to make people more aware of the religious and moral aspects of the possible use of nuclear weapons, aspects that have been neglected even by the churches themselves. This neglect may be the result of fatalism rather than of callousness, but there is time to look again at this fatalism. I shall not suggest to you solutions of the problems that I raise, but I shall suggest a way of thinking about them that, given time, may increase the influences of restraint, reduce the danger of nuclear war, limit the degree of violence in any conflict that may take place, and overcome the tendency to threaten nuclear annihilation whenever there is a crisis that involves the Soviet Union.

First, I shall say a word about the bearing of this lecture on your own nuclear debate. I shall not try to transcend my position as a citizen of the United States, for it is in that capacity that I feel the full force of the nuclear dilemma. I shall often refer to the policies of the government of my country in this lecture, and I know that these policies are not unimportant to you. I do not think what I say will have any special relevance to your debate among yourselves as to whether you should arm your forces with nuclear weapons. Canadians who oppose the possession of nuclear weapons by their own country do not escape from the basic moral dilemma unless they go beyond that and urge unilateral disarmament by the United States as well. So long as they contemplate the American nuclear deterrent as a protection to this continent with even grudging acceptance, you are involved in the same moral problem in which I am involved as an American citizen. You may feel less involved in one way, for you may say that the decision to use these weapons remains in practice with the United States, and some of you may fear that the United States may be more belligerent than you in some situations. At a later point in my lecture I shall mention another point at which you may have similar anxiety. That is the possibility that the United States might initiate the nuclear stage of the war if the NATO powers were threatened by defeat in Europe in a conventional conflict. Awareness of that problem might cause some of you to seek an alternative to nuclear weapons for your own NATO troops. You will have to decide whether this would be useful apart from a general revision of NATO policy.

Whatever you may or may not do about these issues, as an outsider I urge that the most effective Canadian role in international affairs is to be persuasive in representing a point of view about policy that is likely to be slightly different from that of the American government, partly because your government is not subjected to some pressures, such as right wing Congressional committee chairmen, that Washington cannot escape. An element of independence in your foreign policy is good for us all. Pressure from you with regard to steps toward disarmament may well have a salutary effect at the right moment. I have always welcomed the fact that Canada has had an attitude toward Communist China that is different from the American attitude. Though it is difficult to know today what anyone's policy toward China should be, the policy that has aggravated the isolation of China and that has produced almost complete mutual ignorance as between China and the west has been a grievous error.

Whether we approve of it or not, military power is at this time an essential aspect of the power of states and an indispensable condition for the security of nations. Even small nations with little military power of their own depend for their security and freedom on the fact that there is no monopoly of military power in one nation or alliance of nations. I recognize that the phrase "the balance of power" has an evil reputation, and I also know that the balance is always precarious and that nations always seek to upset it in their own favour, but in all of the political relations of men—and even in many other relations—there is need to have power to check power so that no one person or group can impose its will on others. There are many other forms of power that are often more effective than military power, but in the world of nations these cannot achieve full independence of military power. One poignant illustration of this is the present plight of India. India has had many non-military forms of power among the nations, but these seem not to be sufficient to preserve its security or its freedom.

I hope and pray for the time when the power of nations will be modified in two ways. One is radical disarmament so that in any use of military power there will be a great reduction in the degree of the violence to be expected. The other is a better establishment of the rule of law, and the development of the United Nations to the point where it can have effective enough power of its own to keep the peace among the nations. The two are interdependent.

I share with many of you an emotional antipathy to all military power and to all symbols of it, and I also have a moral objection to most uses of military power, but I try to distinguish between these two attitudes. I cannot morally reject all uses of military power. I could not reject its use to defeat Hitler; I could not reject its use in Korea; and I cannot reject its use today against the Chinese invaders of India. Nor can I reject the possession today of deterrent power, even nuclear deterrent power, though this raises grave problems that I shall discuss later.

Our religious traditions have in the main accepted the attitude toward military power that I have expressed. I think that they have generally done so much too uncritically and have wrongly allowed the symbols of religion to be used by nations to support their power, their moral pretensions and their political ambitions. The tradition of the "just war" has been used to limit violence when the weapons were themselves limited; but the more unlimited the weapons, the more inoperative this doctrine of the "just war" has become. Father John Courtney Murray notes the neglect of the doctrine in the Second World War and says, "There is place for an indictment of all of us who failed to make the tradition relevant."[1] I welcome those who are now trying to revive this concept in terms of "limited war" and to relate it to the problems of nuclear war. I have the impression that because Roman Catholic thinkers have the concept of the "just war" as an important part of their tradition, there is more ferment among them on the moral issues of nuclear war than there is among Protestants.

While majority opinion among responsible religious

[1]*Morality and Modern Warfare*, edited by Wm. J. Nagle (Helicon, 1960), p. 84.

thinkers in the west has given moral endorsement to limited uses of military power, there has also been a very impressive pacifist tradition. Pacifists do not like to be told by non-pacifists that they have been an important leaven in the church. They would rather have us all agree with them than praise them. In our time I think that in many Christian circles there has been a very significant shift of the burden of proof in these matters. Through most of Christian history the pacifist has belonged to a minority that was generally disregarded. The American churches even as recently as the First World War showed little respect for the conscientious objector. But we may say that to a considerable extent the burden of proof has shifted to the non-pacifist. Karl Barth puts the matter in this way: "All affirmative answers to the question [of killing in war] are wrong if they do not start with the assumption that the inflexible negative of pacifism has almost infinite arguments in its favour and is almost overpoweringly strong."[1] Notice that he says "almost."

I too have to say "almost," and for two reasons. One is that (under conditions that are now conceivable) pacifism cannot be the policy of a government. A government by its very nature is a trustee for the security and freedom of a nation, and there is no pacifist nation. There may be nations that have almost no armaments, but they must depend upon the protection of a more powerful neighbour or perhaps on some hoped-for action by the United Nations that might involve the use of military force. If pacifist policies are not available for governments, the pacifist himself must have a second-best policy for his government.

The other reason has already been suggested. I think that pacifists—if they insist on something like a pacifist policy for nations, if they deny the place of military power as an essential ingredient of national power, or if they advise

[1] *Church Dogmatics*, III, 4, p. 455.

policies which, while not explicitly pacifistic, have the effect of producing relative military weakness—fail to do justice to the need to prevent a monopoly of military power in any nation or group of nations. They tend to play down the implacable character of some aggressive or tyrannical forces. They trust too much in the power of persuasion, the persuasion of loving example, to resist such evil forces. I realize that there are complications here and that there are pacifists, such as traditional Mennonites and many individuals belonging to other traditions, who have no illusions at this point and choose a strategy of withdrawal from the military aspect of national life, as far as this is possible, as a witness to their faith and not as a solution of a political problem.

I have one other comment on pacifism. I believe that the pacifist witness in the church and in the nation makes a contribution to the sanity of us all, especially if it is not predicated on the assumption that pacifism is a way that is free from the guilt of history. I think that many pacifists realize that they share in the common guilt because their role keeps them from resisting some forms of injustice or tyranny that might be curbed. Professor Roland Bainton, who is himself a pragmatic pacifist, makes a statement at the end of his extremely helpful book *Christian Attitudes toward War and Peace* that seems to me both generous and wise:

At the present juncture there is more need for peace than there is for pacifism. If peace is preserved it will be through the efforts not of pacifists, but of peace-minded nonpacifists, who do not renounce war absolutely, but who oppose war in our time on grounds of the humanitarian and the pragmatic.[1]

In recent years there has been a shift in thinking about the relation of religion and morality to the use of military power once a war has started.[2] I do not mean to suggest that there

[1]Abingdon, 1960, p. 253.
[2]See *The Just War* by Robert W. Tucker (Johns Hopkins Press, 1960), for a discussion of the contrast between American moral restraints in the initiation of war and the lack of restraints when a war is in progress.

has been an explicit renunciation of previously held positions, but there has been a dramatic change in practice concerning what is permitted in war. During the Second World War the obliteration bombing of cities in Germany and Japan—before the use of atomic bombs on Hiroshima and Nagasaki—was an announcement that there are no limits to the violence that is permitted against the enemy at a distance. I put it in this way because I believe that there remained moral inhibitions about what we might do to an individual close at hand whom we could see, though it was assumed to be permissible to incinerate a hundred thousand people, mostly civilians,[1] whom we could not see, in a single night. There were extenuating circumstances. The threat of Hitlerism was so dangerous and so horrible that we felt justified in doing anything to overcome it. Also, very sensitive men believed that the use of the atomic bombs on Japanese cities would make the invasion of Japan unnecessary and thus actually save life. But already the way had been prepared for unlimited violence against populations by the bombing of Hamburg, Dresden, Berlin, Tokyo and other cities. I wonder how much attention was given to the more intangible aspect of the question, to the long-term effect upon us of the fact that we were the nation that first used nuclear bombs on cities without warning. These fateful events in our recent past suggest to me that there was at this point in history a kind of corporate fall (Christian theologians might call it a derivative fall), and that this fall was our terrible preparation for the nuclear age.

I believe that there are still moral inhibitions by which our own nation and many other nations are restrained as they face the possibility of the initiation of war. The renunciation of preventive or pre-emptive war is an illustration of such inhibitions. The Washington correspondent for the *New York Times*,[1] Max Frankel, reported that moral

[1]*New York Times*, Oct. 30, 1962.

inhibitions had an important part in preventing our government from deciding in favour of a military strike against Cuba. In recent years our government has also shown a desire to move away from dependence on threats of massive nuclear retaliation, a desire to have alternatives to both surrender and annihilation.

We may be grateful for all moral restraints in these matters that remain, but I fear that they are secondary to the widespread tendency to assume with fatalism and with an abdication of conscience that military necessity is the ultimate law of life in time of war. I hope that I am wrong, but I cannot resist the conclusion that churches have been swept along by this same tendency. I have heard very little religious or moral criticism of military policies. I have heard a great deal about the strategic considerations that should govern military policy but very little about the moral considerations from the representatives of either church or state. I have heard a great deal about the physical danger that we may be massively destroyed, but I have heard very little about the moral danger that we may be massive destroyers of people in other nations. Perhaps the silence comes more from sheer bafflement than from callousness. If so, this bafflement is in large part a result of the dilemma of nuclear deterrence. I shall now speak about this dilemma.

The dilemma of nuclear deterrence is easily stated. There is a very strong case for possessing nuclear weapons and for expressing the will to use them to deter their use by the other side, but if we ever do use them in a general nuclear war they will destroy most of the things our strategy of deterrence is intended to protect. The dilemma of nuclear deterrence has another dimension. If our possession of nuclear weapons is to deter aggression, the deterrent must be credible in the sense that the potential adversary must *believe* that we will use weapons if he moves beyond a certain point in provocation or aggression. If he is to believe this, it is often contended,

Americans must not show many scruples about nuclear war; they must not do too much debating as to whether we ought to use these weapons.

There was a very striking illustration of this dimension of the dilemma of deterrence in connection with the recent Cuban crisis. I have already referred to Max Frankel's contention in the *New York Times* that moral considerations had an important effect in preventing the President from deciding to attack the Cuban bases or to invade Cuba. This article was reinforced by another day-by-day account of the week of the crisis, in the *Times*, in which the moral argument against such an attack was given considerable emphasis. In response to such reports there appeared in *The Washington Post*[1] an article by Professor Brzezinsky, of Columbia University, one of the leading authorities on the Soviet Union and eastern Europe and a very able representative of the new science of deterrence, which contained the warning that "it is now most unwise to hint or to 'reveal' that the President was not inclined to use force against Cuban missiles, for to do so is to imply to the Soviets that they have been bluffed successfully, and this could have dangerous implications for the future, especially Berlin." This same warning would apply to any debate during the crisis about the morality of such a military attack. It would apply also to any general discussion of the morality of nuclear war in our churches. The nation that shows the fewest scruples about nuclear war can mount the most credible deterrent.

My answer to those who warn against discussion of the moral aspect of nuclear policies is that such silence would leave the field wide open for extremists who are blind or unimaginative concerning the human consequences of nuclear war and who are governed almost entirely by impatience to defeat Communist nations. Policy itself

[1] *The Washington Post*, Nov. 9, 1962.

would get out of balance because public pressures would create a one-sided preoccupation with the danger of Communism to our values and there would be a neglect of the danger of nuclear war to our values. The picture of America among the nations would be a false picture of a nation possessed by nuclear militarism and hell-bent toward everyone's destruction. I can only ask: What would be the effect of this one-sided habit of thinking and feeling on the moral sensitivities of our people? Whatever may be the effect upon the credibility of our policy of deterrence, our churches should seek to overcome any such moral attitude in the nation.

The moral aspects of the problem of nuclear war seem to me to be too much neglected. I do not believe that we can make our decisions about policy or strategy by announcing an abstract absolute which implies its own application in detail to all questions, but I do believe that we should surround the policy-making process with imperatives and warnings.

First, I warn against the prevalent tendency to think of the consequences of nuclear war chiefly in quantitative terms, especially in terms of the number of casualties. We are often told that if we in this country were the victims of a large-scale nuclear attack there would be forty million, eighty million, a hundred and twenty million casualties, the number often depending on whether the writer's advice about provisions for civil defence is heeded. Many of us are familiar with Herman Kahn's brilliant writings on this subject, especially his book entitled *On Thermonuclear War*.[1] Dr. Kahn is right in saying to America that thermonuclear war is possible even though it would be irrational. He is also quite justified in trying to give some idea of what the

[1]Princeton University Press, 1960. Dr. Kahn in more recent statements makes it clear to me that the book represents a kind of abstraction from his full position and that he does at times speak realistically about the consequences of a general nuclear war.

country would be like after an attack. But in doing this he does not take seriously the less tangible effects of a nuclear war. He gives the impression that, given a substantial programme of civil defence, the survivors would be able to re-establish, in a surprisingly short time, a viable nation, free and even prosperous, an embodiment of the old American values. All of this must be radically questioned. I think that Professor Hans Morgenthau, who in his own way is as tough-minded as Herman Kahn, is much nearer to the truth when he says that only one who "is possessed not only by an extreme optimism but by an almost unthinking faith" can believe "that civilization, any civilization, Western or otherwise, could survive such an unprecedented catastrophe."[1] And Reinhold Niebuhr, another inspirer of political realism, doubts if a civilization could survive the monstrous guilt involved in nuclear war.[2]

Is it not probable that a full-scale nuclear war would start a barbaric struggle for survival, of which we had a slight preview in the discussion about the use of guns to keep neighbours out of family shelters? Is it not probable that the fabric of community would be destroyed? Is it not probable that the concern to preserve some kind of order and to find an uncontaminated food supply would have priority for a long time over the concern for freedom or other western values? Walter Lippmann has thus described the probable results of a nuclear war: "It would be followed by a savage struggle for existence as the survivors crawled out of their shelters and the American Republic would be replaced by a stringent military dictatorship trying to keep some kind of order among the desperate survivors."[3] If we think of the results of nuclear war in terms of the number of casualties, it can be argued that it

[1]*Commentary*, Oct. 1961, p. 281.
[2]*Christianity and Crisis*, Nov. 13, 1961.
[3]*New York Herald Tribune*, Sept. 14, 1961.

would be brave for a single generation to absorb the casualties for the sake of freedom. But if freedom is also a casualty,
along with all of the conditions which make for the health
of a community in which freedom can grow, what then are
we to say? If what I have said here is only approximately
true, I think that we can say at least one thing very clearly:
Nuclear war, while we may stumble into it, cannot be
regarded as an instrument of policy. As an instrument of
policy, it can only be self-defeating.

Secondly, I present a moral imperative that has behind it
our religious traditions. Nuclear attacks directed against the
centres of population of another country cannot be justified
either as first strikes or as retaliatory strikes. The threat of
retaliatory strikes is involved in the deterrent, and I realize
that at the present moment it would be difficult for governments to renounce them in advance. At least they may have
to leave the impression that if nuclear war starts, anything
may happen, and this in dealing with rational men would
be a strong deterrent. But whatever may be the ambiguity
in the intentions of governments, it would be apostasy for
our religious communities to give the impression that direct
attacks on populations with hydrogen bombs can under
some circumstances receive religious sanction.

There are many issues here that remain unclear. The old
problem made familiar in Catholic moral theology by the
phrase "double effect" makes it difficult to draw the line
absolutely between an attack on a base and destruction
within a city near the base. There is the further question of
how we distinguish among classes of weapons and especially
between tactical and strategic nuclear weapons. Indeed, the
whole issue may be lost in a debate on these matters. I
find somewhat difficult Professor Paul Ramsey's[1] almost
entire dependence on the distinction between combatants
and non-combatants, though there is real strength in his

[1] *War and the Christian Conscience* (Duke University Press, 1961), *passim.*

contention that every city contains enough persons who are non-combatants—the children and the aged and many whose relation to the war-making power of the enemy is non-existent or marginal—to cause us to spare it from attack. One of my difficulties is that I do not want to give the impression that all limits are off when we think of destroying the drafted armies of young men who have minimal responsibility for any acts of aggression. Strongly as Professor Ramsey argues against it, I think that such considerations as the traditional emphasis upon dispropor-tionate evil and on the need to preserve the powers of recuperation of the enemy nation must guide us as much as the moral principle of the immunity of non-combatants.

The concept of the "just war," understood in these days as "limited war," needs to be revived and made relevant. It should be discussed in the churches, not merely in a few books and articles by moral theologians. Professor Ramsey has done a great service to Protestants in raising the issue so forcefully. There are indications that those who are close to military planning are more concerned about practical ways of limiting violence than are the leaders of the religious communities. And yet even here the achievement on both sides of invulnerable second strike or retaliatory power as the ultimate in deterrence, while it would make for a greater degree of stability, means that if nuclear war were to overtake us, the chief targets would be the centres of population, for the most important military targets would be out of reach.[12]

[12]It is difficult to exaggerate the extent of the moral dilemma that is posed by the view that the surest way to prevent a war in which cities may be bombed is for both sides to secure invulnerable deterrents which, if they should fail to prevent the war, would almost automatically lead to the destruction of cities. There has been much debate over the counter-force strategy set forth in the speech by Secretary MacNamara on June 16, 1962. A counter-force strategy is exactly what those who stress the moral obligation to keep any war limited advocate. Critics of this strategy say that it is very dangerous because it is likely to provoke the enemy to strike first in fear of having his own forces destroyed. They also think that it would make disarmament more difficult

My third suggestion is that we become more alert than we are to the moral issues raised by the possibility of our being the ones to initiate the nuclear stage of a war. The fact that the United States has done this once when it used the bomb in Japan cannot be erased, and it will always haunt us. So far as intentions and expectations for the future are concerned, the United States will not initiate a war by attacking another nation with nuclear weapons. The open question is whether we might initiate the nuclear stage of a war in response to a conventional attack, perhaps in western Europe. The present policy is that under some circumstances we would do this. To keep announcing that we are prepared to do this, both militarily and morally prepared, is part of the deterrent. Those who make these announcements undoubtedly believe that in so doing they are preventing the provocative or aggressive action by the other side that might be the cause of war. At this moment in history they may be right, and what I say is not said in criticism of them in their role. But I think that this whole question is still discussed chiefly in strategic terms and the moral aspects of it are neglected.

---

than would be the case if both sides had the confidence that their retaliatory forces could never be wiped out. It also depends upon a larger force than a strategy that is directed toward the centres of population. Many who take seriously this idea of the invulnerable deterrent desire to have the Soviet Union achieve the same kind of invulnerability for the sake of stability.

As the argument goes, we seem to have to choose between a strategy that is more morally defensible because it is designed to protect centres of population and one that has a better chance of preventing war but that, if it failed to prevent war, would involve the morally indefensible destruction of cities. Quite apart from our planning, if the other side does achieve an invulnerable deterrent, a counter-force strategy would have limited efficacy. Whatever one may say about a short-term justification of the invulnerable-deterrent-counter-cities pattern as the best insurance against war, it seems to me that this pattern itself is insecure, for it could be upset by the initiative of a third party, by a technical accident, or by escalation from a limited military operation. The existence of this dilemma should convince all sides of the moral necessity of radical nuclear disarmament and of finding alternatives to the threat of ultimate violence that is now implicit in any direct encounter between the nuclear powers.

Indeed, a realistic estimate of the effect on the people and the civilization of central Europe where the nuclear weapons might first be used is too little considered. One of the best statements of the effect of the use of nuclear weapons on a limited scale in Europe is to be found in a book by one of the chief advocates of a tough policy in relation to Berlin, Dean Acheson. He says of a limited nuclear war in Europe: "Our allies would see at once that the proposed strategy would consign them to a fate more devastating than would compliance with the demands of the Soviet Union. The merit of this strategy, they would be told, would lie in its avoidance of 'all-out' nuclear war, but it would seem to be all-out enough for them, even though designed to restrain the major participants from battering each other with hydrogen bombs."[1] Mr. Acheson, when he published those words in 1958, put his trust in the effect of the "all-out" nuclear deterrent combined with conventional NATO forces in Europe, an attack on which would be an attack on the United States and thus expose the Soviet Union to our full strategic nuclear power.

There is little doubt that the chief danger of all-out nuclear war in our time is that it may come by way of escalation from some limited military operation. In such a process of escalation it seems still to be true that the line dividing conventional weapons from even small nuclear weapons would be decisive. Professor Henry Kissenger, who was one of the first to emphasize the role of tactical nuclear weapons in western strategy, draws back to some extent from this in his book *The Necessity of Choice*[2] because of the difficulty of avoiding full escalation among nuclear weapons if once the line between conventional and nuclear weapons is crossed. He writes, "The dividing line between conventional and nuclear weapons is more familiar and therefore easier to

[1] *Power and Diplomacy* (Harvard University Press, 1958), p. 98.
[2] Harper, 1960, pp. 82-83.

maintain—assuming the will to do so—than any distinction within the spectrum of nuclear weapons." In view of these considerations, and in view both of the qualitative effects of nuclear war and of the great difficulty in a nuclear war of avoiding massive attacks on populations, I maintain that the United States should not under any circumstances be the one to initiate the nuclear stage of a conflict. This would be a moral choice which we could not defend on the basis of any political advantage. If this contention is sound, an enormous burden is placed on the government to prepare itself for other alternatives. In the meantime, the moral issue is greatly clouded by the fact that most of the people who advocate readiness to initiate the nuclear stage of a war regard this as a strategy of deterrence and are convinced that if we are clear enough about it, the nuclear weapons will not have to be used. This assurance prevents them from facing the full dimensions of the moral problem.

We cannot separate the problems involved in the possession and use of nuclear weapons from the broad context of international relations at this time. The very existence of this ultimate threat to humanity is a grave enough problem for all of us, but the problem is compounded by an ideological conflict which at present makes impossible even minimal mutual trust. We have reason to assume that the Communist powers may seize opportunities to blackmail us into making concessions at the expense of nations now free from Communist control. They have in their history reasons to fear that at some stage an armed Germany might create a situation in which American nuclear power would be used to destroy the Soviet Union. I cannot forget that in 1958 Walter Lippmann came away from a long interview with the conviction that Khrushchev really believed that if the United States found itself losing the cold war, it would start a hot war.[1] Since Khrushchev fully expects the United States to lose the cold war, this prospect may indeed worry him. This is the setting in which we have to deal with the danger of a nuclear holocaust. In my closing words, I shall speak about our attitudes toward this setting.

The chasm between the nations is wider because on the other side governments are committed to atheism, but this should not cause us to regard our nuclear power as a modern form of "a sword for the Lord and for Gideon."[2] There is a temptation to turn the national conflict with Communist nations into a Christian anti-Communist crusade, but to do this would be to corrupt religion and to make the national hostility more fanatical. The religious aspect of the conflict with Communism will go on within nations and across national boundaries, as it goes on today in different ways in Poland, in East Germany, in the Soviet Union and elsewhere, but this religious conflict can be won not with bombs but only by means of religious witness in love. The political struggle against Communist nations tends to separate people; it even tends to separate those of the same faith, for Christians in eastern countries generally do not want to be identified politically with Christians in the west. But the religious struggle for the minds and hearts of men calls for relationships between persons on both sides, for only so can there be witness in love. We do not serve God by allowing religious zeal to make foreign policies so rigid that no accommodations among nations are possible, for such policies would probably lead to the destruction of the people whom God loves on both sides.

If we are patient and succeed in gaining time, we have grounds for hope that diversity in the Communist world and the rise of a less fanatical generation in the Soviet

[1] *New York Herald Tribune,* Nov. 11, 1958.
[2] Judges 7:20 (R.S.V.).

Union will be favourable to peace. Awareness of this real possibility should help us to keep our patience. The force of what I say may be seen best if I put the matter negatively. If we were confronted today by a vast monolithic and unchanging Communist world controlled by the single-minded purpose to impose Communism on all nations, a purpose sustained by an undiminishing fanaticism, there would be, humanly speaking, no hope of avoiding global nuclear war. Just in so far as there are indications that such a picture of the world is untrue, there may be hope of finding alternatives to nuclear war. Variations in the Communist world—not only the Sino-Soviet split, but also the gradations of Communism in eastern Europe from East Germany with its most oppressive Stalinist regime to Poland with its considerable cultural freedom—are of great importance. Changes in the Soviet Union itself, with the passing of the Stalinist terror and with the growing awareness that Russia has so much to lose that it has a great stake in peace, may make all the difference. The fear of being accused of being "soft on Communism" makes it very difficult for the responses of Americans to the Communist world to change with the realities. The one thing of which we can be reasonably sure is that both the Soviet Union and the United States realize that, though there may be no mutual trust between them, they have a paramount mutual interest in preventing war. We knew this before the week of the Cuban crisis, but now we are more vividly aware of it.

The fact that we cannot withdraw unilaterally from the arms race makes it morally imperative to do everything possible in the next period to end nuclear tests and to bring about radical disarmament. We should emphasize not only the risks in every method of disarmament, but also the ultimate risks in the uncontrolled arms race. There will be conflicts within the government of the United States itself on the problems of disarmament, and churches should prepare themselves now to strengthen those groups within government that really believe in disarmament and that are deeply convinced of the risk to humanity as a whole and to national security in the arms race itself.

There needs to be in both of our countries an articulate body of opinion inspired by religious faith, by a sense of solidarity with all men, by respect for God's creation so threatened with the strange blasphemy of destruction by man's new power. This body of opinion would try to understand the world even as it is seen from the other side; would resist the current tendencies to make Communism altogether simple at the very time when, as a human reality, it is becoming highly complex; would know the limits of military power in serving the cause of freedom; would reject the idea of asking once more for the unconditional surrender of our adversaries; would be committed under all conditions to the limitation of violence; would seek to multiply relationships with people behind the Iron Curtain; and would be eager to make the most of the religious ties which we have with many of them. Such a body of opinion, nourished and supported by our churches, would help us to choose not mere survival but life.